The Fast and Easy Air Fryer Cookbook

2000 Days of Healthy and Quick Recipes to Elevate Your Cooking Game

Barbara W. Bolick

Editor: AALIYAH LYONS

Interior Design: BROOKE WHITE

Cover Art: DANIELLE REES

Food stylist: Sienna Adams

Table Of Contents

Introduction

In recent years, the kitchen has seen a culinary revolution with the introduction of a remarkable appliance - the air fryer. These compact kitchen gadgets have taken the culinary world by storm, offering a healthier and more efficient way to cook a wide variety of dishes. If you're looking to make the most of your air fryer, "The Fast and Easy Air Fryer Cookbook" is your ultimate guide, packed with delectable recipes that will transform your cooking experience.

This cookbook not only provides a wide array of mouthwatering recipes but also offers an in-depth introduction to the world of air frying. In this article, we will explore the essentials of this cookbook, starting with what an air fryer is, why you should choose one for your kitchen, and how to use the book effectively.

What Is an Air Fryer?

To get started, it's essential to understand what an air fryer is. An air fryer is a kitchen appliance that uses convection cooking to circulate hot air around food to cook it. This method of cooking mimics the deep-frying process but uses significantly less oil, making it a healthier alternative. The air fryer works by creating a high-temperature, dry environment that surrounds the food, resulting in a crispy exterior and moist interior.

The primary benefits of using an air fryer are evident when it comes to health and convenience. Traditional deep-frying uses a significant amount of oil, which adds extra calories and fat to your meals. In contrast, air frying requires only a minimal amount of oil, or in some cases, no oil at all. This reduction in oil intake can help lower your calorie and fat consumption, making air-fried dishes a healthier choice.

Additionally, air fryers are incredibly versatile and efficient. They can cook a wide range of foods, from vegetables to meats, and even desserts. The cooking process is relatively quick, and the results are often just as satisfying as traditional frying, but without the drawbacks of excessive oil.

Why Choose an Air Fryer?

Now that you understand what an air fryer is, let's delve into why you should consider adding one to your kitchen arsenal.

Healthier Cooking

As previously mentioned, air frying significantly reduces the amount of oil needed for cooking. This not only reduces calorie and fat intake but also minimizes the risks associated with consuming excess oil, such as heart disease and obesity. Air-fried dishes often retain the crispy texture and delicious flavors of deep-fried food without the added health concerns.

Convenience

Air fryers are user-friendly and efficient. They heat up quickly, and most models come with pre-programmed settings for common dishes. This means you can cook a wide variety of meals with minimal effort and time. Plus, the compact size of air fryers makes them ideal for smaller kitchens.

Versatility

Air fryers are not limited to just frying. They can also grill, bake, roast, and even reheat food. This versatility makes them an all-in-one kitchen appliance, reducing the need for multiple cooking tools.

Energy Efficiency

Air fryers are energy-efficient, using less electricity than conventional ovens. This not only saves on your energy bills but also reduces your carbon footprint.

Easy Cleanup

Cleaning an air fryer is a breeze. Most components are dishwasher safe, and the non-stick coatings make it easy to wipe down after use.

Reduced Odors

Traditional frying can leave your kitchen smelling like a fast-food joint. Air frying minimizes odors, keeping your kitchen fresh and clean.

Using "The Fast and Easy Air Fryer Cookbook"

"The Fast and Easy Air Fryer Cookbook" is your key to unlocking the full potential of your air fryer. It's designed to help both beginners and experienced air fryer users explore a world of flavors and possibilities. Here's how to effectively use this cookbook:

Introduction: Start by reading the introduction to the cookbook. This section will give you an overview of what to expect and how the cookbook is organized. Understanding the structure will help you navigate the book with ease.

Equipment and Ingredients: Before you dive into the recipes, make sure you have the necessary equipment and ingredients. Most recipes in this cookbook are designed with common kitchen tools and readily available ingredients in mind. However, you may want to double-check that you have the basics like oil, spices, and common condiments.

Recipe Categories: "The Fast and Easy Air Fryer Cookbook" is likely organized into various sections or categories. These may include appetizers, mains, sides, desserts, and more. Take a moment to explore the table of contents and see which recipes catch your eye.

Recipe Selection: Select a recipe that suits your taste and dietary preferences. One of the beauties of air fryers is their adaptability, so whether you're a meat lover, vegetarian, or looking for healthier options, you'll find something that suits your needs.

Recipe Instructions: The heart of the cookbook lies in the recipe instructions. Each recipe will guide you through the preparation, cooking, and serving steps. Pay close attention to the suggested cooking time and temperature. Since air fryers can vary in their performance, it's essential to keep an eye on your food as it cooks and adjust as needed.

Personalization: Feel free to personalize the recipes to your liking. Experiment with different seasonings, spices, and ingredients to make the dishes your own. The air fryer is incredibly forgiving, allowing for creativity in the kitchen.

Meal Planning: Utilize the cookbook for meal planning. You can create entire menus with recipes from this cookbook, accommodating breakfast, lunch, dinner, and snacks. Plan your meals in advance to make the most of your air fryer and maintain a balanced diet.

Variety: Don't limit yourself to just one or two recipes. "The Fast and Easy Air Fryer Cookbook" likely contains a wide range of recipes, so explore and discover new favorites.

Share the Experience: Cooking with an air fryer can be a fun and social experience. Share your culinary adventures with friends and family, and encourage them to try out the recipes in the cookbook.

In conclusion, "The Fast and Easy Air Fryer Cookbook" is your gateway to a healthier, more efficient, and delicious way of cooking. Understanding what an air fryer is, the reasons to choose one for your kitchen, and how to use the cookbook effectively will set you on a path to culinary success. Embrace the possibilities of air frying, experiment with the recipes in this cookbook, and enjoy the benefits of a kitchen revolution that's here to stay. Happy air frying!

Air Fryer Cooking Chart

Beef					
Item	**Temp (°F)**	**Time (mins)**	**Item**	**Temp (°F)**	**Time (mins)**
Beef Eye Round Roast (4 lbs.)	400 °F	45 to 55	Meatballs (1-inch)	370 °F	7
Burger Patty (4 oz.)	370 °F	16 to 20	Meatballs (3-inch)	380 °F	10
Filet Mignon (8 oz.)	400 °F	18	Ribeye, bone-in (1-inch, 8 oz)	400 °F	10 to 15
Flank Steak (1.5 lbs.)	400 °F	12	Sirloin steaks (1-inch, 12 oz)	400 °F	9 to 14
Flank Steak (2 lbs.)	400 °F	20 to 28			

Chicken					
Item	**Temp (°F)**	**Time (mins)**	**Item**	**Temp (°F)**	**Time (mins)**
Breasts, bone in (1 1/4 lb.)	370 °F	25	Legs, bone-in lb.)	380 °F	30
Breasts, boneless (4 oz)	380 °F	12	Thighs, boneless (1 1/2 lb.)	380 °F	18 to 20
Drumsticks (2 1/2 lb.)	370 °F	20	Wings (2 lb.)	400 °F	12
Game Hen (halved 2 lb.)	390 °F	20	Whole Chicken	360 °F	75
Thighs, bone-in (2 lb.)	380 °F	22	Tenders	360 °F	8 to 10

Pork & Lamb					
Item	Temp (°F)	Time (mins)	Item	Temp (°F)	Time (mins)
Bacon (regular)	400 °F	5 to 7	Pork Tenderloin	370 °F	15
Bacon (thick cut)	400 °F	6 to 10	Sausages	380 °F	15
Pork Loin (2 lb.)	360 °F	55	Lamb Loin Chops (1-inch thick)	400 °F	8 to 12
Pork Chops, bone in (1-inch, 6.5 oz)	400 °F	12	Rack of Lamb (1.5 - lb.)	380 °F	22
Flank Steak (2 lbs.)	400 °F	20 to 28			

Fish & Seafood					
Item	Temp (°F)	Time (mins)	Item	Temp (°F)	Time (mins)
Calamari (8 oz)	400 °F	4	Tuna Steak	400 °F	7 to 10
Fish Fillet (1-inch, 8 oz)	400 °F	10	Scallops	400 °F	5 to 7
Salmon, fillet (6 oz)	380 °F	12	Shrimp	400 °F	5
Swordfish steak	400 °F	10	Sirloin steaks (1-inch, 12 oz)	400 °F	9 to 14
Flank Steak (2 lbs.)	400 °F	20 to 28			

Vegetables					
INGREDIENT	**AMOUNT**	**PREPARATION**	**OIL**	**TEMP**	**COOK TIME**
Asparagus	2 bunches	Cut in half, trim stems	2 Tbsp	420°F	12-15 mins
Beets	1 1/2 lbs	Peel, cut in 1/2-inch cubes	1 Tbsp	390°F	28-30 mins
Bell peppers (for roasting)	4 peppers	Cut in quarters, remove seeds	1 Tbsp	400°F	15-20 mins
Broccoli	1 large head	Cut in 1-2-inch florets	1 Tbsp	400°F	15-20 mins
Brussels sprouts	1 lb	Cut in half, re-move stems	1 Tbsp	425°F	15-20 mins
Carrots	1 lb	Peel, cut in 1/4-inch rounds	1 Tbsp	425°F	10-15 mins
Cauliflower	1 head	Cut in 1-2-inch florets	2 Tbsp	400°F	20-22 mins
Corn on the cob	7 ears	Whole ears, remove husks	1 Tbps	400°F	14-17 mins
Green beans	1 bag (12 oz)	Trim	1 Tbps	420°F	18-20 mins
Kale (for chips)	4 OZ	Tear into pieces, remove stems	None	325°F	5-8 mins
Mushrooms	16 OZ	Rinse, slice thinly	1 Tbps	390°F	25-30 mins
Potatoes, russet	1 1/2 lbs	Cut in 1-inch wedges	1 Tbps	390°F	25-30 mins
Potatoes, russet	1 lb	Hand-cut fries, soak 30 mins in cold water, then pat dry	1/2 -3 Tbps	400°F	25-28 mins
Potatoes, sweet	1 lb	Hand-cut fries, soak 30 mins in cold water, then pat dry	1 Tbps	400°F	25-28 mins
Zucchini	1 lb	Cut in eighths lengthwise, then cut in half	1 Tbps	400°F	15-20 mins

Chapter 1

Appetizers

Cheesy Garlic Bread

Prep time: 5 minutes | Cook time: 15 minutes | Serves 2

- 1 friendly baguette
- 4 tsp. butter, melted
- 3 chopped garlic cloves
- 5 tsp. sundried tomato pesto
- 1 cup mozzarella cheese, grated

1. Cut your baguette into 5 thick round slices.
2. Add the garlic cloves to the melted butter and brush onto each slice of bread.
3. Spread a teaspoon of sun dried tomato pesto onto each slice.
4. Top each slice with the grated mozzarella.
5. Transfer the bread slices to the Air Fryer and cook them at 180°F for 6 – 8 minutes.
6. Top with some freshly chopped basil leaves, chili flakes and oregano if desired.

Keto French Fries

Prep time: 5 minutes | Cook time: 20 minutes | Serves 4

- 1 large rutabaga, peeled, cut into spears about ¼ inch wide
- Salt and pepper to taste
- ½ teaspoon paprika
- 2 tablespoons coconut oil

1. Preheat your air fryer to 450°F.
2. Mix the oil, paprika, salt, and pepper.
3. Pour the oil mixture over the fries, making sure all pieces are well coated.
4. Cook in air fryer for 20-minutes or until crispy.

Crispy Eggplant Fries

Prep time: 5 minutes | Cook time: 12 minutes | Serves 3

- 2 eggplants
- ¼ cup olive oil
- ¼ cup almond flour
- ½ cup water

1. Preheat your air fryer to 390°F.
2. Cut the eggplants into half-inch slices.
3. In a mixing bowl, mix the flour, olive oil, water, and eggplants.
4. Slowly coat the eggplants.
5. Add eggplants to air fryer and cook for 12-minutes.
6. Serve with yogurt or tomato sauce.

Butter Roasted Baby Carrots

Prep time: 20 minutes | Cook time:15 minutes |Serves 4

- 1 pound baby carrots
- 2 tablespoons butter
- Kosher salt and ground white pepper, to taste
- 1 teaspoon paprika
- 1 teaspoon dried oregano

1. Toss the carrots with the remaining ingredients | then, arrange the carrots in the Air Fryer cooking basket.
2. Cook the carrots at 380 °F for 15 minutes, shaking the basket halfway through the cooking time.
3. Bon appétit!

Ham and Cheese Stuffed Serrano Peppers

Prep time: 10 minutes | Cook time:7 minutes |Serves 4

- 8 Serrano peppers
- 4 ounces ham cubes
- 4 ounces goat cheese, crumbled

1. Stuff the peppers with ham and cheese | transfer them to a lightly oiled Air Fryer basket.
2. Air fry the peppers at 370 °For about 7 minutes or until golden brown.
3. Bon appétit!

Gruyere Cheese-Stuffed Poblanos

Prep time: 10 minutes | Cook time:7 minutes |Serves 4

- 8 poblano peppers, seeded and halved
- 4 ounces Gruyere cheese
- 4 ounces bacon, chopped

1. Stuff the peppers with the cheese and bacon | transfer them to a lightly oiled Air Fryer basket.
2. Air fry the peppers at 370 °For about 7 minutes or until golden brown.
3. Bon appétit!

Classic Kale Chips

Prep time: 10 minutes | Cook time:8 minutes |Serves 4

- 4 cups kale, torn into pieces
- 1 tablespoon sesame oil
- 1 teaspoon garlic powder
- Sea salt and ground black pepper, to taste

1. Start by preheating your Air Fryer to 360 °F.
2. Toss the kale leaves with the remaining

ingredients and place them in the Air Fryer cooking basket.
3. Air fry your chips for 8 minutes, shaking the basket occasionally and working in batches.
4. Enjoy!

Cheesy Zucchini Chips

Prep time: 15 minutes | Cook time:10 minutes |Serves 4

- 1 pound zucchini, sliced
- 1 cup Pecorino Romano cheese, grated
- Sea salt and cayenne pepper, to taste

1. Start by preheating your Air Fryer to 390 °F.
2. Toss the zucchini slices with the remaining ingredients and arrange them in a single layer in the Air Fryer cooking basket.
3. Cook the zucchini slices for about 10 minutes at 390 °F, shaking the basket halfway through the cooking time. Work in batches.
4. Bon appétit!

Charred Shishito Peppers

Prep time: 5 minutes | Cook time:5 minutes

|Serves 4

- 20 shishito peppers (about 6 ounces)
- 1 teaspoon vegetable oil
- coarse sea salt
- 1 lemon

1. Pre-heat the air fryer to 390°F.
2. Toss the shishito peppers with the oil and salt. You can do this in a bowl or directly in the air fryer basket.
3. Air-fry at 390°F for 5 minutes, shaking the basket once or twice while they cook.
4. Turn the charred peppers out into a bowl. Squeeze some lemon juice over the top and season with coarse sea salt. These should be served as finger foods – pick the pepper up by the stem and eat the whole pepper, seeds and all. Watch for that surprise spicy one!

Tuscan Tomato Toast

Prep time: 5 minutes | Cook time: 5 minutes |

Makes 2 toasts

- 1½ teaspoons extra-virgin olive oil
- 1 teaspoon Tuscan Herb Mix (this page)
- 2 slices Italian-style bread, cut to ½ x 3 x 6 inches
- ⅓–½ cup sundried tomatoes, coarsely chopped or torn
- 1 slice vegan provolone cheese

1. In a small bowl, stir the olive oil and Tuscan Herb Mix together.
2. Brush the seasoned oil on one side of the bread.
3. Cover the surface of each unoiled side of bread with the sundried tomatoes and top with cheese.
4. Cook at 390°F for 5–8 minutes, until the bottom of bread has toasted and the

cheese has melted.

Smoky Sandwich

Prep time: 5 minutes | Cook time: 8 minutes |

Makes 2 sandwiches

- 4 slices whole-grain bread
- 4 slices provolone-style vegan cheese
- 2 slices meatless hickory-smoked deli slices
- olive oil for misting

1. Lay 2 slices of bread on a cutting board.
2. On each slice of bread, layer 1 slice of vegan cheese, one deli slice, the other cheese slice, then top with the other slice of bread.
3. Mist both sides of the sandwich with oil.
4. Cut each sandwich into rectangular halves.
5. Place in the air fryer basket and cook at 390°F for 5 to 8 minutes, until the bread toasts.

Green Cabbage with Mint

Prep time: 10 minutes | Cook time: 5 minutes |

Serves 2

- 1/2 green cabbage
- 1 package fresh mint
- 1 minced garlic clove
- 1 lemon
- 1 pinch salt

1. Wash and cut the cabbage and mint roughly.
2. Sauté garlic and salt in a pan with 500ml of water and cook in an air fryer for 20 minutes.
3. Serve and enjoy!

Roasted Nuts

Prep time: 1 minutes | Cook time: 7 minutes | Makes 1 cup

- 1 cup blanched whole almonds

1. Preheat the air fryer to 360°F.
2. Place the nuts in the air fryer basket.
3. Cook the nuts for 3 minutes.
4. Stop and shake the basket. Continue cooking for 2 to 4 more minutes or until the nuts brown to your liking.

Honey Roasted Carrots

Prep time: 5 minutes | Cook time: 25 minutes | Serves 4

- 3 cups baby carrots
- 1 tablespoon olive oil
- 1 tablespoon honey
- Salt and pepper to taste

1. Toss all the ingredients in a bowl.
2. Cook for 12-minutes in an air fryer at 390°F.

Skinny Fries

Prep time: 5 minutes | Cook time:30 minutes |Serves 2

- 2 to 3 russet potatoes,
- peeled and cut into ¼-inch sticks
- 2 to 3 teaspoons olive or vegetable oil
- Salt

1. Cut the potatoes into ¼-inch strips. (A mandolin with a julienne blade is really helpful here.) Rinse the potatoes with cold water several times and let them soak in cold water for at least 10 minutes or as long as overnight.
2. Pre-heat the air fryer to 380°F.
3. Drain and dry the potato sticks really well, using a clean kitchen towel. Toss the

fries with the oil in a bowl and then air-fry the fries in two batches at 380°F for 15 minutes, shaking the basket a couple of times while they cook.
4. Add the first batch of French fries back into the air fryer basket with the finishing batch and let everything warm through for a few minutes. As soon as the fries are done, season them with salt and transfer to a plate or basket. Serve them warm with ketchup or your favorite dip.

Tortilla Chips

Prep time: 2 minutes | Cook time: 5 minutes | Serves 2

- 8 corn tortillas
- Salt to taste
- 1 tbsp. olive oil

1. Pre-heat your Air Fryer to 390°F.
2. Slice the corn tortillas into triangles. Coat with a light brushing of olive oil.
3. Put the tortilla pieces in the wire basket and air fry for 3 minutes. You may need to do this in multiple batches.
4. Season with salt before serving.

Sweet Potato Fries

Prep time: 15 minutes | Cook time: 15 minutes | Serves 3-4

- 3 large sweet potatoes
- 1 tablespoon light olive oil
- 1 tablespoon dried tarragon
- salt and pepper
- cinnamon sugar (optional)

1. Cut the sweet potatoes into fries, 1/4 x 3 inches. (Peeling the potatoes is optional.)
2. Toss the fries, oil, and tarragon together and stir to coat completely.
3. Pour the fries into the air fryer basket and cook at 390°F for 5 minutes.
4. Stir or shake the basket and cook for 5 more minutes, until the fries brown.
5. Season to taste with salt and pepper or cinnamon sugar.

Cinnamon Apple Chips

Prep time: 15 minutes | Cook time:9 minutes | Serves 4

- 2 large sweet, crisp apples, cored and sliced
- 1 teaspoon ground cinnamon
- 1/2 teaspoon grated nutmeg
- A pinch of salt

1. Start by preheating your Air Fryer to 390 °F.
2. Toss the apple slices with the remaining ingredients and arrange them in a single layer in the Air Fryer cooking basket.
3. Cook the apple chips for about 9 minutes at 390 °F, shaking the basket halfway through the cooking time. Work in batches.
4. Bon appétit!

Classic Yam Chips

Prep time: 20 minutes | Cook time:15 minutes |Serves 2

- 1 large-sized yam, peeled and cut into 1/4-inch sticks
- 1 tablespoon olive oil
- Kosher salt and red pepper, to taste

1. Start by preheating your Air Fryer to 360 °F.
2. Toss the yam with the remaining ingredients and place them in the Air Fryer cooking basket.
3. Air fry the yam sticks for 15 minutes, tossing halfway through the cooking time and working in batches.
4. Enjoy!

Hot and Spicy Tortilla Chips

Prep time: 10 minutes | Cook time:5 minutes |Serves 4

- 9 corn tortillas, cut into wedges
- 1 tablespoon olive oil
- 1 teaspoon hot paprika
- Sea salt and ground black pepper, to taste

1. Toss the tortilla wedges with the remaining ingredients.
2. Cook your tortilla chips at 360 °F for about 5 minutes or until crispy. Work in batches.
3. Enjoy!

Tortilla Strips

Prep time: 5 minutes | Cook time: 5 minutes | Serves 4

- 10 (6- to 8-inch) corn tortillas
- oil for misting

1. Mist each tortilla, front and back, with oil and stack.
2. Cut the tortillas into 1/4 x 1 1/2-inch strips.
3. Place all the strips in the air fryer basket and cook at 390°F for 5 minutes.
4. Stir and cook for 2 more minutes, until they brown and become crispy.

Tomato & Avocado Egg Rolls

Prep time: 5 minutes | Cook time: 15 minutes | Serves 5

- 10 egg roll wrappers
- 3 avocados, peeled and pitted
- 1 tomato, diced
- Salt and pepper, to taste

1. Pre-heat your Air Fryer to 350°F.
2. Put the tomato and avocados in a bowl. Sprinkle on some salt and pepper and mash together with a fork until a smooth consistency is achieved.
3. Spoon equal amounts of the mixture onto the wrappers. Roll the wrappers around the filling, enclosing them entirely.
4. Transfer the rolls to a lined baking dish and cook for 5 minutes.

Puppy Poppers

Prep time: 5 minutes | Cook time: 20 minutes | Serves 50 treats

- 1/2 cup unsweetened applesauce
- 1 cup peanut butter
- 2 cup oats
- 1 cup flour
- 1 tsp. baking powder

1. Combine the applesauce and peanut butter in a bowl to create a smooth consistency.
2. Pour in the oats, flour and baking powder. Continue mixing to form a soft dough.
3. Shape a half-teaspoon of dough into a ball and continue with the rest of the dough.
4. Pre-heat the Air Fryer to 350°F.
5. Grease the bottom of the basket with oil.
6. Place the poppers in the fryer and cook for 8 minutes, flipping the balls at the halfway point. You may need to cook the poppers in batches.
7. Let the poppers cool and serve immediately or keep in an airtight container for up to 2 weeks.

Chapter 2

Breakfasts

Green Scramble

Prep time:5 minutes |Cook time: 20 minutes |Serves 4

- 1 tablespoon olive oil
- ½ teaspoon smoked paprika
- 12 eggs, whisked
- 3 cups baby spinach
- Salt and black pepper to the taste

1. In a bowl, mix all the ingredients except the oil and whisk them well.
2. Heat up your air fryer at 360 °F, add the oil, heat it up, add the eggs and spinach mix, cover, cook for 20 minutes, divide between plates and serve.

Pancakes

Prep time: 5 minutes | Cook time: 10 minutes | Serves 2

- 2 tbsp coconut oil
- 1 tsp maple extract
- 2 tbsp cashew milk
- 2 eggs
- 2/3 oz/20g pork rinds

1. Grind up the pork rinds until fine and mix with the rest of the ingredients, except the oil.
2. Add the oil to a skillet. Add a quarter-cup of the batter and fry until golden on each side. Continue adding the remaining batter.

Mixed Peppers Hash

Prep time:5 minutes |Cook time: 20 minutes |Serves 4

- 1 red bell pepper, cut into strips
- 1 green bell pepper, cut into strips
- 1 orange bell pepper, cut into strips
- 4 eggs, whisked
- Salt and black pepper to the taste

- 2 tablespoons mozzarella, shredded Cooking spray

1. In a bowl, mix the eggs with all the bell peppers, salt and pepper and toss.
2. Preheat the air fryer at 350 °F, grease it with cooking spray, pour the eggs mixture, spread well, sprinkle the mozzarella on top and cook for 20 minutes.
3. Divide between plates and serve for breakfast.

Cinnamon Toasts

Prep time: 5 minutes | Cook time: 10 minutes | Serves 4

- 10 bread slices
- 1 pack salted butter
- 4 tbsp. sugar
- 2 tsp. ground cinnamon
- ½ tsp. vanilla extract

1. In a bowl, combine the butter, cinnamon, sugar, and vanilla extract. Spread onto the slices of bread.
2. Set your Air Fryer to 380°F. When warmed up, put the bread inside the fryer and cook for 4 – 5 minutes.

Hash Brown

Prep time: 5 minutes | Cook time: 15 minutes | Serves 2

- 12 oz grated fresh cauliflower (about ½ a medium-sized head)
- 4 slices bacon, chopped
- 3 oz onion, chopped
- 1 tbsp butter, softened

1. In a skillet, sauté the bacon and onion until brown.
2. Add in the cauliflower and stir until tender and browned.
3. Add the butter steadily as it cooks.
4. Season to taste with salt and pepper.
5. Enjoy!

Eggs Ramekins

Prep time:5 minutes |Cook time: 6 minutes |Serves 5

- 5 eggs
- 1 teaspoon coconut oil, melted
- ¼ teaspoon ground black pepper

1. Brush the ramekins with coconut oil and crack the eggs inside.
2. Then sprinkle the eggs with ground black pepper and transfer in the air fryer.
3. Cook the baked eggs for 6 minutes at 355F.

Seasoned Herbed Sourdough Croutons

Prep time: 5 minutes | Cook time:5 to 7 minutes |Serves 4

- 4 cups cubed sourdough bread, 1-inch cubes (about 8 ounces)
- 1 tablespoon olive oil
- 1 teaspoon fresh thyme leaves
- ¼ – ½ teaspoon salt

- freshly ground black pepper

1. Combine all ingredients in a bowl and taste to make sure it is seasoned to your liking.
2. Pre-heat the air fryer to 400°F.
3. Toss the bread cubes into the air fryer and air-fry for 5 to 7 minutes, shaking the basket once or twice while they cook.
4. Serve warm or store in an airtight container.

Basil Tomato Bowls

Prep time:5 minutes |Cook time: 15 minutes |Serves 4

- 1 pound cherry tomatoes, halved
- 1 cup mozzarella, shredded Cooking spray
- Salt and black pepper to the taste
- 1 teaspoon basil, chopped

1. Grease the tomatoes with the cooking spray, season with salt and pepper, sprinkle the mozzarella on top, place them all in your air fryer's basket, cook at 330 °F for 15 minutes, divide into bowls, sprinkle the basil on top and serve.

Egg Muffin Sandwich

Prep time: 3 minutes | Cook time: 12 minutes | Serves 1

- 1 egg
- 2 slices bacon
- 1 English muffin

1. Pre-heat your Air Fryer at 395°F
2. Take a ramekin and spritz it with cooking spray. Break an egg into the ramekin before transferring it to the basket of your fryer, along with the English muffin and bacon slices, keeping each component separate.
3. Allow to cook for 6 minutes. After removing from the fryer, allow to cool for around two minutes. Halve the muffin.
4. Create your sandwich by arranging the egg and bacon slices on the base and topping with the other half of the muffin.

Spanish Omelet

Prep time: 5 minutes | Cook time: 10 minutes | Serves 2

- 3 eggs
- Cayenne or black pepper
- ½ cup finely chopped vegetables of your choosing.

1. In a pan on high heat, stir-fry the vegetables in extra virgin olive oil until lightly crispy.
2. Cook the eggs with one tablespoon of water and a pinch of pepper.
3. When almost cooked, top with the vegetables and flip to cook briefly.
4. Serve.

Bacon & Eggs

Prep time: 2 minutes | Cook time: 3 minutes | Serves 1

- Parsley
- Cherry tomatoes
- 1/3 oz/150g bacon
- eggs

1. Fry up the bacon and put it to the side.
2. Scramble the eggs in the bacon grease, with some pepper and salt. If you want, scramble in some cherry tomatoes. Sprinkle with some parsley and enjoy.

Paprika Zucchini Spread

Prep time:5 minutes |Cook time: 15 minutes |Serves 4

- 4 zucchinis, roughly chopped
- 1 tablespoon sweet paprika
- Salt and black pepper to the taste
- 1 tablespoon butter, melted

1. Grease a baking pan that fits the Air Fryer with the butter, add all the ingredients, toss, and cook at 360 °F for 15 minutes.
2. Transfer to a blender, pulse well, divide into bowls and serve for breakfast.

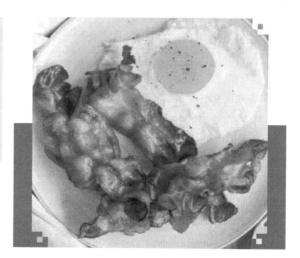

Parsley Omelet

Prep time:5 minute |Cook time: 15 minutes |Serves 4

- 4 eggs, whisked
- 1 tablespoon parsley, chopped
- ½ teaspoons cheddar cheese, shredded
- 1 avocado, peeled, pitted and cubed Cooking spray

1. In a bowl, mix all the ingredients except the cooking spray and whisk well.
2. Grease a baking pan that fits the Air Fryer with the cooking spray, pour the omelet mix, spread, introduce the pan in the machine and cook at 370 °F for 15 minutes.
3. Serve for breakfast.

Peanut Butter Bread

Prep time: 5 minutes | Cook time: 10 minutes | Serves 3

- 1 tbsp. oil
- 2 tbsp. peanut butter
- 4 slices bread
- 1 banana, sliced

1. Spread the peanut butter on top of each slice of bread, then arrange the banana slices on top. Sandwich two slices together, then the other two.
2. Oil the inside of the Air Fryer and cook the bread for 5 minutes at 300°F.

Spinach Spread

Prep time:5 minutes |Cook time: 10 minutes |Serves 4

- 2 tablespoons coconut cream
- 3 cups spinach leaves
- 2 tablespoons cilantro
- 2 tablespoons bacon, cooked and crumbled
- Salt and black pepper to the taste

1. In a pan that fits the air fryer, combine all the ingredients except the bacon, put the pan in the machine and cook at 360 °F for 10 minutes.
2. Transfer to a blender, pulse well, divide into bowls and serve with bacon sprinkled on top.

Garlic Bread Knots

Prep time: 5 minutes | Cook time:10 minutes |Serves 8

- ¼ cup melted butter
- 2 teaspoons garlic powder
- 1 teaspoon dried parsley
- 1 (11-ounce) tube of refrigerated French bread dough

1. Mix the melted butter, garlic powder and dried parsley in a small bowl and set it aside.
2. To make smaller knots, cut the long tube of bread dough into 16 slices. If you want to make bigger knots, slice the dough into 8 slices. Shape each slice into a long rope about 6 inches long by rolling it on a flat surface with the palm of your hands. Tie each rope into a knot and place them on a plate.
3. Pre-heat the air fryer to 350°F.
4. Transfer half of the bread knots into the air fryer basket, leaving space in between each knot. Brush each knot with the butter mixture using a pastry brush.
5. Air-fry for 5 minutes. Remove the baked knots and brush a little more of the garlic butter mixture on each. Repeat with the remaining bread knots and serve warm.

Coconut Berries Bowls

Prep time:5 minutes |Cook time: 15 minutes |Serves 4

- 1 and ½ cups coconut milk
- ½ cup blackberries
- 2 teaspoon stevia
- ½ cup coconut, shredded

1. In your air fryer's pan, mix all the ingredients, stir, cover and cook at 360 °F for 15 minutes.
2. Divide into bowls and serve for breakfast.

Breakfast Sandwich

Prep time: 5 minutes | Cook time: 5 minutes | Serves 1

- 2 oz/60g cheddar cheese
- 1/6 oz/30g smoked ham
- 2 tbsp butter
- 4 eggs

1. Fry all the eggs and sprinkle the pepper and salt on them.
2. Place an egg down as the sandwich base. Top with the ham and cheese and a drop or two of Tabasco.
3. Place the other egg on top and enjoy.

Cheese Eggs and Leeks

Prep time:5 minutes |Cook time: 7 minutes |Serves 2

- 2 leeks, chopped
- 4 eggs, whisked
- ¼ cup Cheddar cheese, shredded
- ½ cup Mozzarella cheese, shredded
- 1 teaspoon avocado oil

1. Preheat the air fryer to 400F.
2. Then brush the air fryer basket with avocado oil and combine the eggs with the rest of the ingredients inside.
3. Cook for 7 minutes and serve.

Chapter 3

Poultry

Pesto Chicken

Prep time:10 minutes |Cook time: 25 minutes |Serves 4

- 12 oz chicken legs
- 1 teaspoon sesame oil
- ½ teaspoon chili flakes
- 4 teaspoons pesto sauce

1. In the shallow bowl mix up pesto sauce, chili flakes, and sesame oil.
2. Then rub the chicken legs with the pesto mixture.
3. Preheat the air fryer to 390F.
4. Put the chicken legs in the air fryer basket and cook them for 25 minutes.

Fried Herbed Chicken Wings

Prep time:10 minutes |Cook time: 11 minutes |Serves 4

- 1 tablespoon Emperor herbs chicken spices
- 8 chicken wings
- Cooking spray

1. Generously sprinkle the chicken wings with Emperor herbs chicken spices and place in the preheated to 400F air fryer.
2. Cook the chicken wings for 6 minutes from each side.

Balsamic Duck and Cranberry Sauce

Prep time:5 minutes |Cook time: 25 minutes |Serves 4

- 4 duck breasts, boneless, skin-on and scored Apinch of salt and black pepper
- 1 tablespoon olive oil
- ¼ cup balsamic vinegar
- ½ cup dried cranberries

1. Heat up a pan that fits your air fryer with

the oil over medium-high heat, add the duck breasts skin side down and cook for 5 minutes.
2. Add the rest of the ingredients, toss, put the pan in the fryer and cook at 380 °F for 20 minutes.
3. Divide between plates and serve.

Greek Chicken Meatballs

Prep time: 3 minutes | Cook time: 15 minutes | Serves 1

- ½ oz. finely ground pork rinds
- 1 lb. ground chicken
- 1 tsp. Greek seasoning
- 1/3 cup feta, crumbled
- 1/3 cup frozen spinach, drained and thawed

1. Place all the ingredients in a large bowl and combine using your hands. Take equal-sized portions of this mixture and roll each into a 2-inch ball. Place the balls in your fryer.
2. Cook the meatballs at 350°F for twelve minutes, in several batches if necessary.
3. Once they are golden, ensure they have reached an ideal temperature of 165°F and remove from the fryer. Keep each batch warm while you move on to the next one. Serve with Tzatziki if desired.

Crispy Chicken

Prep time: 2 minutes | Cook time: 8 minutes | Serves 2

- 1 lb. chicken skin
- 1 tsp. butter
- ½ tsp. chili flakes
- 1 tsp. dill

1. Pre-heat the fryer at 360°F.
2. Cut the chicken skin into slices.
3. Heat the butter until melted and pour it over the chicken skin. Toss with chili flakes, dill, and any additional seasonings to taste, making sure to coat well.
4. Cook the skins in the fryer for three minutes. Turn them over and cook on the other side for another three minutes.
5. Serve immediately or save them for later – they can be eaten hot or at room temperature.

Cinnamon Balsamic Duck

Prep time:5 minutes |Cook time: 20 minutes |Serves 2

- 2 duck breasts, boneless and skin scored Apinch of salt and black pepper
- ¼ teaspoon cinnamon powder
- 4 tablespoons stevia
- 3 tablespoons balsamic vinegar

1. In a bowl, mix the duck breasts with the rest of the ingredients and rub well.
2. Put the duck breasts in your air fryer's basket and cook at 380 °F for 10 minutes on each side.
3. Divide everything between plates and serve.

Smoked Paprika Chicken Cutlets

Prep time: 20 minutes | Cook time:12 minutes |Serves 4

- 1 pound chicken breasts, boneless, skinless, cut into 4 pieces
- 1 tablespoon butter, melted
- 1 teaspoon smoked paprika
- Kosher salt and ground black pepper, to taste
- 1 teaspoon garlic powder

1. Flatten the chicken breasts to 1/4-inch thickness.
2. Toss the chicken breasts with the remaining ingredients.
3. Cook the chicken at 380 °F for 12 minutes, turning them over halfway through the cooking time.
4. Bon appétit!

Coconut Turkey and Spinach Mix

Prep time:5 minutes |Cook time: 15 minutes |Serves 4

- 1 pound turkey meat, ground and browned
- 1 tablespoon garlic, minced
- 1 tablespoon ginger, grated
- 2 tablespoons coconut aminos
- 4 cups spinach leaves Apinch of salt and black pepper

1. In a pan that fits your air fryer, combine all the ingredients and toss.
2. Put the pan in the air fryer and cook at 380 °F for 15 minutes Divide everything into bowls and serve.

Crispy Chicken Wings

Prep time: 15 minutes | Cook time:18 minutes |Serves 4

- 3/4 pound chicken wings, boneless
- 1 tablespoon butter, room temperature
- 1/2 teaspoon garlic powder
- 1/2 teaspoon shallot powder
- 1/2 teaspoon mustard powder

1. Toss the chicken wings with the remaining ingredients.
2. Cook the chicken wings at 380 °F for 18 minutes, turning them over halfway through the cooking time.
3. Bon appétit!

Mozzarella Turkey Rolls

Prep time: 3 minutes | Cook time: 20 minutes | Serves 4

- 4 slices turkey breast
- 1 cup sliced fresh mozzarella
- 1 tomato, sliced
- ½ cup fresh basil
- 4 chive shoots

1. Pre-heat your Air Fryer to 390°F.
2. Lay the slices of mozzarella, tomato and basil on top of each turkey slice.
3. Roll the turkey up, enclosing the filling well, and secure by tying a chive shoot around each one.
4. Put in the Air Fryer and cook for 10 minutes. Serve with a salad if desired.

Hot Chicken Thighs

Prep time: 25 minutes | Cook time:22 minutes |Serves 4

- 1 pound chicken thighs, bone-in
- Sea salt and freshly ground black pepper, to taste
- 2 tablespoons olive oil

- 1 teaspoon stone-ground mustard
- 1/4 cup hot sauce

1. Pat the chicken dry with kitchen towels. Toss the chicken with the remaining ingredients.
2. Cook the chicken at 380 °F for 22 minutes, turning them over halfway through the cooking time.
3. Bon appétit!

Charcoal Chicken

Prep time: 3 minutes | Cook time: 20 minutes | Serves 2

- 2 medium skinless, boneless chicken breasts
- ½ tsp. salt
- 3 tbsp. Cajun spice
- 1 tbsp. olive oil

1. Massage the salt and Cajun spice into the chicken breasts. Drizzle with olive oil.
2. Pre-heat the Air Fryer to 370°F.
3. Place the chicken in the fryer and cook for 7 minutes.
4. Flip both chicken breasts over and cook for an additional 3 – 4 minutes.
5. Slice up before serving.

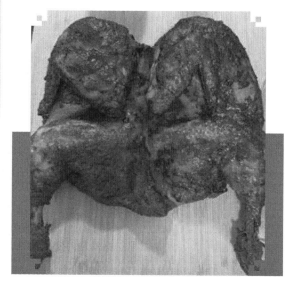

Traditional Orange Duck

Prep time: 45 minutes | Cook time:40 minutes |Serves 4

- 1 pound duck legs
- 1/4 cup orange sauce
- Sea salt and red pepper flakes, crushed

1. Toss the duck legs with the remaining ingredients.
2. Cook the duck legs at 400 °F for 40 minutes, turning them over halfway through the cooking time.
3. Bon appétit!

Cajun Seasoned Chicken

Prep time: 2 minutes | Cook time: 13 minutes | Serves 2

- 2 boneless chicken breasts
- 3 tbsp. Cajun spice

1. Coat both sides of the chicken breasts with Cajun spice. Put the seasoned chicken in Air Fryer basket.
2. Air fry at 350°F for 10 minutes, ensuring they are cooked through before slicing up and serving.

Rustic Duck Fillet

Prep time: 40 minutes | Cook time:15 minutes |Serves 4

- 1 ½ pounds duck fillet
- 1 tablespoon honey
- 2 tablespoons dark soy sauce
- 1 tablespoon soybean paste

1. Toss the duck fillets with the remaining ingredients.
2. Cook the duck fillets at 330 °F for 15 minutes, turning them over halfway through the cooking time.
3. Turn the heat to 350 °F | continue to cook for about 15 minutes or until cooked through.
4. Let it rest for 10 minutes before carving and serving. Bon appétit!

Balsamic Chicken Drumettes

Prep time: 25 minutes | Cook time:22 minutes |Serves 4

- 1 ½ pounds chicken drumettes
- 2 tablespoons olive oil
- 2 tablespoons balsamic vinegar
- Kosher salt and ground black pepper, to taste

1. Toss the chicken drumettes with the remaining ingredients.
2. Cook the chicken drumettes at 380 °F for 22 minutes, turning them over halfway through the cooking time.
3. Bon appétit!

Bacon-Wrapped Chicken

Prep time: 2 minutes | Cook time: 20 minutes | Serves 6

- 1 chicken breast, cut into 6 pieces
- 6 rashers back bacon
- 1 tbsp. soft cheese

1. Put the bacon rashers on a flat surface and cover one side with the soft cheese.
2. Lay the chicken pieces on each bacon rasher. Wrap the bacon around the chicken and use a toothpick stick to hold each one in place. Put them in Air Fryer basket.
3. Air fry at 350°F for 15 minutes.

Chicken & Pepperoni Pizza

Prep time: 3 minutes | Cook time: 17 minutes | Serves 6

- 2 cups cooked chicken, cubed
- 20 slices pepperoni
- 1 cup sugar-free pizza sauce
- 1 cup mozzarella cheese, shredded
- ¼ cup parmesan cheese, grated

1. Place the chicken into the base of a four-cup baking dish and add the pepperoni and pizza sauce on top. Mix well so as to completely coat the meat with the sauce.
2. Add the parmesan and mozzarella on top of the chicken, then place the baking dish into your fryer.
3. Cook for 15 minutes at 375°F.
4. When everything is bubbling and melted, remove from the fryer. Serve hot.

Chives and Lemon Chicken

Prep time:5 minutes |Cook time: 20 minutes |Serves 4

- 1 pound chicken tenders, boneless, skinless Apinch of salt and black pepper
- Juice of 1 lemon
- 1 tablespoon chives, chopped Adrizzle of olive oil

1. In a bowl, mix the chicken tenders with all ingredients except the chives, toss, put the meat in your air fryer's basket and cook at 370 °F for 10 minutes on each side.
2. Divide between plates and serve with chives sprinkled on top.

Asian-Style Duck

Prep time: 40minutes | Cook time:15 minutes |Serves 3

- 1 pound duck breast
- 1 tablespoon Hoisin sauce
- 1 tablespoon Five-spice powder
- Sea salt and black pepper, to taste
- 1/4 teaspoon ground cinnamon

1. Pat the duck breasts dry with paper towels. Toss the duck breast with the remaining ingredients.
2. Cook the duck breast at 330 °F for 15 minutes, turning them over halfway through the cooking time.
3. Turn the heat to 350 °F | continue to cook for about 15 minutes or until cooked through.
4. Let it rest for 10 minutes before carving and serving. Bon appétit!

Buttery Turkey and Mushroom Sauce

Prep time:5 minutes |Cook time: 25 minutes |Serves 4

- 6 cups leftover turkey meat, skinless, boneless and shredded Apinch of salt and black pepper
- 1 tablespoon parsley, chopped
- 1 cup chicken stock
- 3 tablespoons butter, melted
- 1 pound mushrooms, sliced
- 2 spring onions, chopped

1. Heat up a pan that fits the air fryer with the butter over medium-high heat, add the mushrooms and sauté for 5 minutes.
2. Add the rest of the ingredients, toss, put the pan in the machine and cook at 370 °F for 20 minutes.
3. Divide everything between plates and serve.

Almond Coconut Chicken Tenders

Prep time:5 minutes |Cook time: 20 minutes |Serves 4

- 4 chicken breasts, skinless, boneless and cut into tenders Apinch of salt and black pepper
- 1/3 cup almond flour
- 2 eggs, whisked
- 9 ounces coconut flakes

1. Season the chicken tenders with salt and pepper, dredge them in almond flour, then dip in eggs and roll in coconut flakes.
2. Put the chicken tenders in your air fryer's basket and cook at 400 °F for 10 minutes on each side.
3. Divide between plates and serve with a side salad.

Pepper Turkey Bacon

Prep time:10 minutes |Cook time: 8 minutes |Serves 2

- 7 oz turkey bacon
- 1 teaspoon coconut oil, melted
- ½ teaspoon ground black pepper

1. Slice the turkey bacon if needed and sprinkle it with ground black pepper and coconut oil.
2. Preheat the air fryer to 400F.
3. Arrange the turkey bacon in the air fryer in one layer and cook it for 4 minutes.
4. Then flip the bacon on another side and cook for 4 minutes more.

Tomato Chicken Mix

Prep time:10 minutes |Cook time: 18 minutes |Serves 4

- 1-pound chicken breast, skinless, boneless
- 1 tablespoon keto tomato sauce
- 1 teaspoon avocado oil
- ½ teaspoon garlic powder

1. In the small bowl mix up tomato sauce, avocado oil, and garlic powder.
2. Then brush the chicken breast with the tomato sauce mixture well.
3. Preheat the air fryer to 385F.
4. Place the chicken breast in the air fryer and cook it for 15 minutes.
5. Then flip it on another side and cook for 3 minutes more.
6. Slice the cooked chicken breast into servings.

Garlic Chicken Wings

Prep time:5 minutes |Cook time: 30 minutes |Serves 4

- 2 pounds chicken wings
- ¼ cup olive oil
- Juice of 2 lemons
- Zest of 1 lemon, grated Apinch of salt and black pepper
- 2 garlic cloves, minced

1. In a bowl, mix the chicken wings with the rest of the ingredients and toss well.
2. Put the chicken wings in your air fryer's basket and cook at 400 °F for 30 minutes, shaking halfway.
3. Divide between plates and serve with a side salad.

Chapter 4

Beef, Pork and Lamb

Creamy Pork Mix

Prep time:5 minutes |Cook time: 25 minutes |Serves 4

- 1 pound pork stew meat, cubed
- 4 teaspoons sweet paprika Apinch of salt and black pepper
- 1 cup coconut cream
- 1 tablespoon butter, melted
- 1 tablespoon parsley, chopped

1. Heat up a pan that fits the air fryer with the butter over medium heat, add the meat and brown for 5 minutes.
2. Add the remaining ingredients, toss, put the pan in the air fryer, cook at 390 °F for 20 minutes more, divide into bowls and serve.

Rosemary Steaks

Prep time:5 minutes |Cook time: 24 minutes |Serves 4

- 4 rib eye steaks Apinch of salt and black pepper
- 1 tablespoon olive oil
- 1 teaspoon sweet paprika
- 1 teaspoon cumin, ground
- 1 teaspoon rosemary, chopped

1. In a bowl, mix the steaks with the rest of the ingredients, toss and put them in your air fryer's basket.
2. Cook at 380 °F for 12 minutes on each side, divide between plates and serve.

Bacon Wrapped Filets Mignons

Prep time: 5 minutes | Cook time:18 minutes |Serves 4

- 4 slices bacon (not thick cut)
- 4 (8-ounce) filets mignons
- 1 tablespoon fresh thyme leaves
- salt and freshly ground black pepper

1. Pre-heat the air fryer to 400°F.
2. Lay the bacon slices down on a cutting board and sprinkle the thyme leaves on the bacon slices. Remove any string tying the filets and place the steaks down on their sides on top of the bacon slices. Roll the bacon around the side of the filets and secure the bacon to the fillets with a toothpick or two.
3. Season the steaks generously with salt and freshly ground black pepper and transfer the steaks to the air fryer.
4. Air-fry for 18 minutes, turning the steaks over halfway through the cooking process. This should cook your steaks to about medium, depending on how thick they are. If you'd prefer your steaks medium-rare or medium-well, simply add or subtract two minutes from the cooking time. Remove the steaks from the air fryer and let them rest for 5 minutes before removing the toothpicks and serving.

Minty Lamb Mix

Prep time:5 minutes |Cook time: 24 minutes |Serves 4

- 8 lamb chops Apinch of salt and black pepper
- 1 cup mint, chopped
- 1 garlic clove, minced
- Juice of 1 lemon
- 2 tablespoons olive oil

1. In a blender, combine all the ingredients except the lamb and pulse well.
2. Rub lamb chops with the mint sauce, put them in your air fryer's basket and cook at 400 °F for 12 minutes on each side.
3. Divide everything between plates and serve.

Garlic Dill Leg of Lamb

Prep time:15 minutes |Cook time: 21 minutes |Serves 2

- 9 oz leg of lamb, boneless
- 1 teaspoon minced garlic
- 2 tablespoons butter, softened
- ½ teaspoon dried dill
- ½ teaspoon salt

1. In the shallow bowl mix up minced garlic, butter, dried dill, and salt.
2. Then rub the leg of lamb with butter mixture and place it in the air fryer.
3. Cook it at 380F for 21 minutes.

Blue Cheese Pork Loin Filets

Prep time: 20 minutes | Cook time:10 minutes |Serves 4

- 1 ½ pounds pork loin filets
- Sea salt and ground black pepper, to taste
- 2 tablespoons olive oil
- 1 pound mushrooms, sliced

- 2 ounces blue cheese

1. Place the pork, salt, black pepper, and olive oil in a lightly greased Air Fryer cooking basket.
2. Cook the pork loin filets at 400 °F for 10 minutes, turning them over halfway through the cooking time.
3. Top the pork loin filets with the mushrooms. Continue to cook for about 5 minutes longer. Top the warm pork with blue cheese.
4. Bon appétit!

Roasted Lamb

Prep time:5 minutes |Cook time: 30 minutes |Serves 4

- 8 lamb cutlets
- 2 tablespoons olive oil Apinch of salt and black pepper
- 2 tablespoons rosemary, chopped
- 2 garlic cloves, minced Apinch of cayenne pepper

1. In a bowl, mix the lamb with the rest of the ingredients and rub well.
2. Put the lamb in the fryer's basket and cook at 380 °F for 30 minutes, flipping them halfway.
3. Divide the cutlets between plates and serve.

Hot Paprika Beef

Prep time:5 minutes |Cook time: 20 minutes |Serves 4

- 1 tablespoon hot paprika
- 4 beef steaks
- Salt and black pepper to the taste
- 1 tablespoon butter, melted

1. In a bowl, mix the beef with the rest of the ingredients, rub well, transfer the steaks to your air fryer's basket and cook at 390 °F for 10 minutes on each side.
2. Divide the steaks between plates and serve with a side salad.

Montreal Ribeye Steak

Prep time: 20 minutes | Cook time:15 minutes |Serves 4

- 1 ½ pounds ribeye steak, bone-in
- 2 tablespoons butter
- 1 Montreal seasoning mix
- Sea salt and ground black pepper, to taste

1. Toss the ribeye steak with the remaining ingredients | place the ribeye steak in a lightly oiled Air Fryer cooking basket.
2. Cook the ribeye steak at 400 °F for 15 minutes, turning it over halfway through the cooking time.
3. Bon appétit!

Holiday Pork Belly

Prep time: 50 minutes | Cook time:20 minutes |Serves 5

- 1 pound pork belly
- 1 tablespoon tomato sauce
- 2 tablespoons rice vinegar
- 1 teaspoon dried thyme
- 1 teaspoon dried rosemary

1. Toss all ingredients in a lightly greased Air Fryer cooking basket.
2. Cook the pork belly at 320 °F for 20 minutes. Now, turn it over and continue cooking for a further 25 minutes.
3. Serve warm and enjoy!

Restaurant-Style Beef Burgers

Prep time: 20 minutes | Cook time:15 minutes |Serves 3

- 3/4 pound ground beef
- 2 cloves garlic, minced
- 1 small onion, chopped
- Kosher salt and ground black pepper, to taste
- 3 hamburger buns

1. Mix the beef, garlic, onion, salt, and black pepper until everything is well combined. Form the mixture into three patties.
2. Cook the burgers at 380 °F for about 15 minutes or until cooked through | make sure to turn them over halfway through the cooking time.
3. Serve your burgers on the prepared buns and enjoy!

Sesame Lamb Chops

Prep time:10 minutes |Cook time: 11 minutes |Serves 6

- 6 lamb chops (3 oz each lamb chop)
- 1 tablespoon sesame oil
- 1 tablespoon za'atar seasonings

1. Rub the lamb chops with za'atar seasonings and sprinkle with sesame oil.
2. Preheat the air fryer to 400F.
3. Then arrange the lamb chops in the air fryer in one layer and cook them for 5 minutes.
4. Then flip the pork chops on another side and cook them for 6 minutes more.

Classic Italian Sausage Sandwich

Prep time: 20 minutes | Cook time:15 minutes |Serves 2

- 1 pound sweet Italian sausage
- 6 white bread slices
- 2 teaspoons mustard

1. Place the sausage in a lightly greased Air fryer cooking basket.
2. Air fry the sausage at 370 °F for approximately 15 minutes, tossing the basket halfway through the cooking time.
3. Assemble the sandwiches with the bread, mustard, and sausage, and serve immediately.
4. Bon appétit!

Butter Beef

Prep time:10 minutes |Cook time: 10 minutes |Serves 4

- 4 beef steaks (3 oz each steak)
- 4 tablespoons butter, softened

- 1 teaspoon ground black pepper
- ½ teaspoon salt

1. In the shallow bowl mix up softened butter, ground black pepper, and salt.
2. Then brush the beef steaks with the butter mixture from each side.
3. Preheat the air fryer to 400F.
4. Put the butter steaks in the air fryer and cook them for 5 minutes from each side.

Paprika Flank Steak

Prep time: 15 minutes | Cook time:12 minutes |Serves 5

- 2 pounds flank steak
- 2 tablespoons olive oil
- 1 teaspoon paprika
- Sea salt and ground black pepper, to taste

1. Toss the steak with the remaining ingredients | place the steak in the Air Fryer cooking basket.
2. Cook the steak at 400 °F for 12 minutes, turning over halfway through the cooking time.
3. Bon appétit!

Burger Patties

Prep time: 2 minutes | Cook time: 13 minutes | Serves 6

- 1 lb. ground beef
- 6 cheddar cheese slices
- Pepper and salt to taste

1. Pre-heat the Air Fryer to 350°F.
2. Sprinkle the salt and pepper on the ground beef.
3. Shape six equal portions of the ground beef into patties and put each one in the Air Fryer basket.
4. Air fry the patties for 10 minutes.
5. Top the patties with the cheese slices and air fry for one more minute.
6. Serve the patties on top of dinner rolls.

Frankfurter Sausage with Honey and Beer

Prep time: 20 minutes | Cook time:15 minutes |Serves 4

- 1 pound Frankfurter sausage
- 1/4 cup ginger ale
- 2 tablespoons liquid honey
- Red pepper flakes, to taste

1. Place all ingredients in a lightly greased Air Fryer cooking basket.
2. Air fry the sausage at 370 °F for approximately 15 minutes, tossing the basket halfway through the cooking time.
3. Bon appétit!

Rosemary Ribeye Steak

Prep time: 20 minutes | Cook time:15 minutes |Serves 4

- 1 pound ribeye steak, bone-in
- 2 tablespoons butter, room temperature
- 2 garlic cloves, minced

- Sea salt and ground black pepper, to taste
- 2 rosemary sprigs, leaves picked, chopped

1. Toss the ribeye steak with the butter, garlic, salt, black pepper, and rosemary | place the steak in the Air Fryer cooking basket.
2. Cook the ribeye steak at 400 °F for 15 minutes, turning it over halfway through the cooking time.
3. Bon appétit!

Fried Steak

Prep time: 2 minutes | Cook time: 13 minutes | Serves 1

- 3 cm-thick beef steak
- Pepper and salt to taste

1. Pre-heat the Air Fryer 400°F for 5 minutes.
2. Place the beef steak in the baking tray and sprinkle on pepper and salt.
3. Spritz the steak with cooking spray.
4. Allow to cook for 3 minutes. Turn the steak over and cook on the other side for 3 more minutes. Serve hot.

Beef and Spring Onions

Prep time:5 minutes |Cook time: 15 minutes |Serves 2

- 2 cups corned beef, cooked and shredded
- 2 garlic cloves, minced
- 1 pound radishes, quartered
- 2 spring onions, chopped Apinch of salt and black pepper

1. In a pan that fits your air fryer, mix the beef with the rest of the ingredients, toss, put the pan in the fryer and cook at 390 °F for 15 minutes.
2. Divide everything into bowls and serve.

Basil Pork

Prep time:5 minutes |Cook time: 25 minutes |Serves 4

- 4 pork chops Apinch of salt and black pepper
- 2 teaspoons basil, dried
- 2 tablespoons olive oil
- ½ teaspoon chili powder

1. In a pan that fits your air fryer, mix all the ingredients, toss, introduce in the fryer and cook at 400 °F for 25 minutes.
2. Divide everything between plates and serve.

Balsamic Pork Chops

Prep time:5 minutes |Cook time: 25 minutes |Serves 4

- 4 pork chops
- 1 tablespoon smoked paprika
- 1 tablespoon olive oil
- 2 tablespoons balsamic vinegar
- ½ cup chicken stock Apinch of salt and black pepper

1. In a bowl, mix the pork chops with the rest of the ingredients and toss.
2. Put the pork chops in your air fryer's basket and cook at 390 °F for 25 minutes.
3. Divide between plates and serve.

Chapter 5

Fish & Seafood

Cod and Sauce

Prep time:5 minutes |Cook time: 15 minutes |Serves 2

- 2 cod fillets, boneless
- Salt and black pepper to the taste
- 1 bunch spring onions, chopped
- 3 tablespoons ghee, melted

1. In a pan that fits the air fryer, combine all the ingredients, toss gently, introduce in the air fryer and cook at 360 °F for 15 minutes.
2. Divide the fish and sauce between plates and serve.

Lime Cod

Prep time:5 minutes |Cook time: 14 minutes |Serves 4

- 4 cod fillets, boneless
- 1 tablespoon olive oil
- Salt and black pepper to the taste
- 2 teaspoons sweet paprika
- Juice of 1 lime

1. In a bowl, mix all the ingredients, transfer the fish to your air fryer's basket and cook 350 °F for 7 minutes on each side.
2. Divide the fish between plates and serve with a side salad.

Easy Orange Roughy Fillets

Prep time: 15 minutes | Cook time:10 minutes |Serves 4

- 1 pound orange roughy fillets
- 2 tablespoons butter
- 2 cloves garlic, minced
- Sea salt and red pepper flakes, to taste

1. Toss the fish fillets with the remaining ingredients and place them in a lightly oiled Air Fryer cooking basket.

2. Cook the fish fillets at 400 °F for about 10 minutes, turning them over halfway through the cooking time.
3. Bon appétit!

Crab Legs

Prep time: 5 minutes | Cook time: 15 minutes | Serves 3

- 3 lb. crab legs
- ¼ cup salted butter, melted and divided
- ½ lemon, juiced
- ¼ tsp. garlic powder

1. In a bowl, toss the crab legs and two tablespoons of the melted butter together. Place the crab legs in the basket of the fryer.
2. Cook at 400°F for fifteen minutes, giving the basket a good shake halfway through.
3. Combine the remaining butter with the lemon juice and garlic powder.
4. Crack open the cooked crab legs and remove the meat. Serve with the butter dip on the side and enjoy!

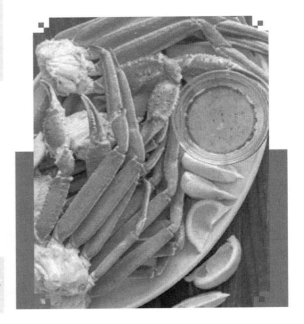

Coconut Shrimp

Prep time: 5 minutes | Cook time: 12 minutes | Serves 4

- 1 tablespoon ghee, melted
- 1 pound shrimp, peeled and deveined
- ¼ cup coconut cream Apinch of red pepper flakes Apinch of salt and black pepper
- 1 tablespoon parsley, chopped
- 1 tablespoon chives, chopped

1. In a pan that fits the fryer, combine all the ingredients except the parsley, put the pan in the fryer and cook at 360 °F for 12 minutes.
2. Divide the mix into bowls, sprinkle the parsley on top and serve.

Lemon Shrimp and Zucchinis

Prep time: 5 minutes | Cook time: 15 minutes | Serves 4

- 1 pound shrimp, peeled and deveined Apinch of salt and black pepper
- 2 zucchinis, cut into medium cubes
- 1 tablespoon lemon juice
- 1 tablespoon olive oil
- 1 tablespoon garlic, minced

1. In a pan that fits the air fryer, combine all the ingredients, toss, put the pan in the machine and cook at 370 °F for 15 minutes.
2. Divide between plates and serve right away.

Mustard Cod

Prep time: 10 minutes | Cook time: 14 minutes | Serves 4

- 1 cup parmesan, grated
- 4 cod fillets, boneless
- Salt and black pepper to the taste

- 1 tablespoon mustard

1. In a bowl, mix the parmesan with salt, pepper and the mustard and stir.
2. Spread this over the cod, arrange the fish in the air fryer's basket and cook at 370 °F for 7 minutes on each side.
3. Divide between plates and serve with a side salad.

Shrimp and Parsley Olives

Prep time: 5 minutes | Cook time: 12 minutes | Serves 4

- 1 pound shrimp, peeled and deveined
- 4 garlic clove, minced
- 1 cup black olives, pitted and chopped
- 3 tablespoons parsley
- 1 tablespoon olive oil

1. In a pan that fits the air fryer, combine all the ingredients, toss, put the pan in the machine and cook at 380 °F for 12 minutes.
2. Divide between plates and serve.

Butter Lobster

Prep time:10 minutes |Cook time: 6 minutes |Serves 4

- 4 lobster tails, peeled
- 4 teaspoons almond butter
- ½ teaspoon salt
- ½ teaspoon dried thyme
- 1 tablespoon avocado oil

1. Make the cut on the back of every lobster tail and sprinkle them with dried thyme and salt.
2. After this, sprinkle the lobster tails with avocado oil.
3. Preheat the air fryer to 380F.
4. Place the lobster tails in the air fryer basket and cook them for 5 minutes.
5. After this, gently spread the lobster tails with almond butter and cook for 1 minute more.

Ghee Shrimp and Green Beans

Prep time:5 minutes |Cook time: 15 minutes |Serves 4

- 1 pound shrimp, peeled and deveined Apinch of salt and black pepper
- ½ pound green beans, trimmed and halved
- Juice of 1 lime
- 2 tablespoons cilantro, chopped
- ¼ cup ghee, melted

1. In a pan that fits your air fryer, mix all the ingredients, toss, introduce in the fryer and cook at 360 °F for 15 minutes shaking the fryer halfway.
2. Divide into bowls and serve.

Parmesan Monkfish Fillets

Prep time: 15 minutes | Cook time:14 minutes |Serves 4

- 1 pound monkfish fillets

- Coarse sea salt and ground black pepper, to taste
- 2 tablespoons butter
- 2 tablespoons lemon juice
- 4 tablespoon Parmesan cheese, grated

1. Toss the fish fillets with the remaining ingredients, except for the Parmesan cheese | place them in a lightly oiled Air Fryer cooking basket.
2. Cook the fish fillets at 400 °F for about 14 minutes, turning them over halfway through the cooking time.
3. Top the fish fillets with the grated Parmesan cheese and serve immediately. Bon appétit!

Italian Shrimp

Prep time:3 minutes |Cook time: 12 minutes |Serves 4

- 1 pound shrimp, peeled and deveined Apinch of salt and black pepper
- 1 tablespoon sesame seeds, toasted
- ½ teaspoon Italian seasoning
- 1 tablespoon olive oil

1. In a bowl, mix the shrimp with the rest of the ingredients and toss well.
2. Put the shrimp in the air fryer's basket, cook at 370 °F for 12 minutes, divide into bowls and serve.

Breadcrumbed Fish

Prep time: 5 minutes | Cook time: 25 minutes | Serves 2 – 4

- 4 tbsp. vegetable oil
- 5 oz. friendly bread crumbs
- 1 egg
- 4 medium fish fillets

1. Pre-heat your Air Fryer to 350°F.
2. In a bowl, combine the bread crumbs and oil.
3. In a separate bowl, stir the egg with a whisk. Dredge each fish fillet in the egg before coating it in the crumbs mixture. Put them in Air Fryer basket.
4. Cook for 12 minutes and serve hot.

Broiled Tilapia

Prep time: 3 minutes | Cook time: 7 minutes | Serves 4

- 1 lb. tilapia fillets
- ½ tsp. lemon pepper
- Salt to taste

1. Spritz the Air Fryer basket with some cooking spray.
2. Put the tilapia fillets in basket and sprinkle on the lemon pepper and salt.
3. Cook at 400°F for 7 minutes.
4. Serve with a side of vegetables.

Spicy Mackerel

Prep time: 5 minutes | Cook time: 15 minutes | Serves 2

- 2 mackerel fillets
- 2 tbsp. red chili flakes
- 2 tsp. garlic, minced
- 1 tsp. lemon juice

1. Season the mackerel fillets with the red pepper flakes, minced garlic, and a drizzle of lemon juice. Allow to sit for five minutes.
2. Preheat your fryer at 350°F.
3. Cook the mackerel for five minutes, before opening the drawer, flipping the fillets, and allowing to cook on the other side for another five minutes.
4. Plate the fillets, making sure to spoon any remaining juice over them before serving.

Crusty Pesto Salmon

Prep time: 5 minutes | Cook time: 10 minutes | Serves 2

- ¼ cup s, roughly chopped
- ¼ cup pesto
- 2 x 4-oz. salmon fillets
- 2 tbsp. unsalted butter, melted

1. Mix the s and pesto together.
2. Place the salmon fillets in a round baking dish, roughly six inches in diameter.
3. Brush the fillets with butter, followed by the pesto mixture, ensuring to coat both the top and bottom. Put the baking dish inside the fryer.
4. Cook for twelve minutes at 390°F.
5. The salmon is ready when it flakes easily when prodded with a fork. Serve warm.

Italian-Style Sea Bass

Prep time: 15 minutes | Cook time:10 minutes |Serves 4

- 1 pound sea bass
- 2 garlic cloves, minced
- 2 tablespoons olive oil
- 1 tablespoon Italian seasoning mix
- Sea salt and ground black pepper, to taste
- 1/4 cup dry white wine

1. Toss the fish with the remaining ingredients | place them in a lightly oiled Air Fryer cooking basket.
2. Cook the fish at 400 °F for about 10 minutes, turning them over halfway through the cooking time.
3. Bon appétit!

Fried Crawfish

Prep time:10 minutes |Cook time: 5 minutes |Serves 4

- 1-pound crawfish
- 1 tablespoon avocado oil
- 1 teaspoon onion powder
- 1 tablespoon rosemary, chopped

1. Preheat the air fryer to 340F.
2. Place the crawfish in the air fryer basket and sprinkle with avocado oil and rosemary.
3. Add the onion powder and stir the crawfish gently.
4. Cook the meal for 5 minutes.

Parmesan Salmon Fillets

Prep time:5 minutes |Cook time: 15 minutes |Serves 4

- 4 salmon fillets, skinless
- 1 teaspoon mustard Apinch of salt and black pepper
- ½ cup coconut flakes

- 1 tablespoon parmesan, grated Cooking spray

1. In a bowl, mix the parmesan with the other ingredients except the fish and cooking spray and stir well.
2. Coat the fish in this mix, grease it with cooking spray and arrange in the air fryer's basket.
3. Cook at 400 °F for 15 minutes, divide between plates and serve with a side salad.

Stevia Cod

Prep time:5 minutes |Cook time: 15 minutes |Serves 4

- 1/3 cup stevia
- 2 tablespoons coconut aminos
- 4 cod fillets, boneless
- A pinch of salt and black pepper

1. In a pan that fits the air fryer, combine all the ingredients and toss gently.
2. Introduce the pan in the fryer and cook at 350 °F for 14 minutes, flipping the fish halfway.
3. Divide everything between plates and serve.

Chapter 6

Side Dishes and Snacks

Coconut Chives Sprouts

Prep time:5 minutes |Cook time: 20 minutes |Serves 4

- 1 pound Brussels sprouts, trimmed and halved
- Salt and black pepper to the taste
- 2 tablespoons ghee, melted
- ½ cup coconut cream
- 2 tablespoons garlic, minced
- 1 tablespoon chives, chopped

1. In your air fryer, mix the sprouts with the rest of the ingredients except the chives, toss well, introduce in the air fryer and cook them at 370 °F for 20 minutes.
2. Divide the Brussels sprouts between plates, sprinkle the chives on top and serve as a side dish.

Lemon Fennel

Prep time:5 minutes |Cook time: 15 minutes |Serves 4

- 1 pound fennel, cut into small wedges Apinch of salt and black pepper
- 3 tablespoons olive oil
- Salt and black pepper to the taste
- Juice of ½ lemon
- 2 tablespoons sunflower seeds

1. In a bowl, mix the fennel wedges with all the ingredients except the sunflower seeds, put them in your air fryer's basket and cook at 400 °F for 15 minutes.
2. Divide the fennel between plates, sprinkle the sunflower seeds on top, and serve as a side dish.

Garlic Radishes

Prep time:5 minutes |Cook time: 15 minutes |Serves 4

- 20 radishes, halved
- 1 teaspoon chives, chopped
- 1 tablespoon garlic, minced
- Salt and black pepper to the taste
- 2 tablespoons olive oil

1. In your air fryer's pan, combine all the ingredients and toss.
2. Introduce the pan in the machine and cook at 370 °F for 15 minutes.
3. Divide between plates and serve as a side dish.

Sage Artichoke

Prep time:10 minutes |Cook time: 12 minutes |Serves 4

- 4 artichokes
- 1 tablespoon sage
- 4 teaspoons avocado oil
- 1 teaspoon chives, chopped
- ½ teaspoon salt

1. Cut the artichoke into halves and rub them with sage avocado oil, minced garlic, and salt.
2. Preheat the air fryer to 375F.
3. Place the artichoke halves in the air fryer basket and cook them for 12 minutes.

Roasted Onions

Prep time: 5 minutes | Cook time:10 to 15 minutes |Serves 1

- 1 onion, sliced or cut into ¾-inch chunks
- olive oil
- salt and freshly ground black pepper

1. Pre-heat the air fryer to 350°F.
2. Toss the onion in a bowl with a little olive oil, salt and freshly ground black pepper.
3. Transfer the onion to the air fryer basket and air-fry for 10 to 15 minutes (depending on how tender you'd like them to be), shaking the basket a few times during the cooking process.

Parmesan Zucchini Chips

Prep time: 3 minutes | Cook time: 10 minutes | Serves 1

- 2 medium zucchini
- 1 oz. pork rinds, finely ground
- ½ cup parmesan cheese, grated
- 1 egg

1. Cut the zucchini into slices about a quarter-inch thick. Lay on a paper towel to dry.
2. In a bowl, combine the ground pork rinds and the grated parmesan.
3. In a separate bowl, beat the egg with a fork.
4. Take a zucchini slice and dip it into the egg, then into the pork rind-parmesan mixture, making sure to coat it evenly. Repeat with the rest of the slices. Lay them in the basket of your fryer, taking care not to overlap. This step may need to be completed in more than one batch.
5. Cook at 320°F for five minutes. Turn the chips over and allow to cook for another five minutes.

6. Allow to cool to achieve a crispier texture or serve warm. Enjoy!

Crust-less Meaty Pizza

Prep time: 3 minutes | Cook time: 15 minutes | Serves 1

- ½ cup mozzarella cheese, shredded
- 2 slices sugar-free bacon, cooked and crumbled
- ¼ cup ground sausage, cooked
- 7 slices pepperoni
- 1 tbsp. parmesan cheese, grated

1. Spread the mozzarella across the bottom of a six-inch cake pan. Throw on the bacon, sausage, and pepperoni, then add a sprinkle of the parmesan cheese on top. Place the pan inside your air fryer.
2. Cook at 400°F for five minutes. The cheese is ready once brown in color and bubbly. Take care when removing the pan from the fryer and serve.

Granny's Green Beans

Prep time: 3 minutes | Cook time: 10 minutes |
Serves 4

- 1 lb green beans, trimmed
- 1 cup butter
- 2 cloves garlic, minced
- 1 cup toasted pine nuts

1. Boil a pot of water.
2. Add the green beans and cook until tender for 5 minutes.
3. Heat the butter in a large skillet over a high heat. Add the garlic and pine nuts and sauté for 2 minutes or until the pine nuts are lightly browned.
4. Transfer the green beans to the skillet and turn until coated.
5. Serve!

Bacon-Wrapped Sausage Skewers

Prep time: 2 minutes | Cook time: 8 minutes |
Serves 2

- 5 Italian chicken sausages
- 10 slices bacon

1. Preheat your air fryer to 370°F/190°C.
2. Cut the sausage into four pieces.
3. Slice the bacon in half. Wrap the bacon over the sausage. Skewer the sausage.
4. Fry for 4-5 minutes until browned.

Brussels Sprouts with Cheese Sauce

Prep time: 2 minutes | Cook time: 10 minutes |
Serves 2

- ¾ cups Brussels sprouts
- 1 tbsp. extra virgin olive oil
- ¼ tsp. salt
- ¼ cup mozzarella cheese, shredded

1. Halve the Brussels sprouts and drizzle with the olive oil. Season with salt and toss to coat.
2. Pre-heat your fryer at 375°F. When warm, transfer the Brussels sprouts inside and add the shredded mozzarella on top.
3. Cook for five minutes, serving when the cheese is melted.

Buffalo Cauliflower

Prep time: 2 minutes | Cook time: 10 minutes |
Serves 1

- ½ packet dry ranch seasoning
- 2 tbsp. salted butter, melted
- Cauliflower florets
- ¼ cup buffalo sauce

1. In a bowl, combine the dry ranch seasoning and butter. Toss with the cauliflower florets to coat and transfer them to the fryer.
2. Cook at 400°F for five minutes, shaking the basket occasionally to ensure the florets cook evenly.
3. Remove the cauliflower from the fryer, pour the buffalo sauce over it, and enjoy.

Bacon Green Beans Mix

Prep time:15 minutes |Cook time: 13 minutes |Serves 4

- 1 cup green beans, trimmed
- 4 oz bacon, sliced
- ¼ teaspoon salt
- 1 tablespoon avocado oil

1. Wrap the green beans in the sliced bacon.
2. After this, sprinkle the vegetables with salt and avocado oil.
3. Preheat the air fryer to 385F.
4. Carefully arrange the green beans in the air fryer in one layer and cook them for 5 minutes.
5. Then flip the green beans on another side and cook for 8 minutes more.

Butter Fennel

Prep time:5 minutes |Cook time: 12 minutes |Serves 4

- 2 big fennel bulbs, sliced
- 2 tablespoons butter, melted
- Salt and black pepper to the taste
- ½ cup coconut cream

1. In a pan that fits the air fryer, combine all the ingredients, toss, introduce in the machine and cook at 370 °F for 12 minutes.
2. Divide between plates and serve as a side dish.

Hot Broccoli

Prep time:5 minutes |Cook time: 5 minutes |Serves 4

- 11 oz broccoli stems
- 1 tablespoon olive oil
- ¼ teaspoon chili powder

1. Preheat the air fryer to 400F.
2. Then chop the broccoli stems roughly and sprinkle with chili powder and olive oil.
3. Transfer the greens in the preheated air fryer and cook them for 5 minutes.

Paprika Green Beans

Prep time:5 minutes |Cook time: 20 minutes |Serves 4

- 6 cups green beans, trimmed
- 2 tablespoons olive oil
- 1 tablespoon hot paprika Apinch of salt and black pepper

1. In a bowl, mix the green beans with the other ingredients, toss, put them in the air fryer's basket and cook at 370 °F for 20 minutes.
2. Divide between plates and serve as a side dish.

Basil Squash

Prep time:5 minutes |Cook time: 10 minutes |Serves 4

- 1 teaspoon sesame oil
- 1 teaspoon dried basil
- 6 oz Kabocha squash, roughly chopped

1. Sprinkle the squash with dried basil and sesame oil and place it in the air fryer basket.
2. Cook the vegetables at 400F for 4 minutes.
3. Then shake them well and cook for 6 minutes more.
4. The time of cooking depends on kabocha squash size.

Chapter 7

Vegan & Vegetarian

Avocado and Cabbage Salad

Prep time:5 minutes |Cook time: 15 minutes |Serves 4

- 2 cups red cabbage, shredded Adrizzle of olive oil
- 1 red bell pepper, sliced
- 1 small avocado, peeled, pitted and sliced
- Salt and black pepper to the taste

1. Grease your air fryer with the oil, add all the ingredients, toss, cover and cook at 400 °F for 15 minutes.
2. Divide into bowls and serve cold for breakfast.

Green Beans Salad

Prep time:5 minutes |Cook time: 15 minutes |Serves 4

- 1 and ¾ cups radishes, chopped
- ½ pound green beans, trimmed Apinch of salt and black pepper
- 4 eggs, whisked Cooking spray
- 1 tablespoon cilantro, chopped

1. Grease a pan that fits the air fryer with the cooking spray, add all the ingredients, toss and cook at 360 °F for 15 minutes.
2. Divide between plates and serve for breakfast.

Chili Lime Broccoli

Prep time:5 minutes |Cook time: 15 minutes |Serves 4

- 1 pound broccoli florets
- 2 tablespoons olive oil
- 2 tablespoons chili sauce
- Juice of 1 lime Apinch of salt and black pepper

1. In a bowl, mix the broccoli with the other ingredients and toss well.
2. Put the broccoli in your air fryer's basket and cook at 400 °F for 15 minutes.
3. Divide between plates and serve.

Paprika Asparagus

Prep time:5 minutes |Cook time: 10 minutes |Serves 4

- 1 pound asparagus, trimmed
- 3 tablespoons olive oil Apinch of salt and black pepper
- 1 tablespoon sweet paprika

1. In a bowl, mix the asparagus with the rest of the ingredients and toss.
2. Put the asparagus in your air fryer's basket and cook at 400 °F for 10 minutes.
3. Divide between plates and serve.

Taco Okra

Prep time:10 minutes |Cook time: 10 minutes |Serves 3

- 9 oz okra, chopped
- 1 teaspoon taco seasoning
- 1 teaspoon sunflower oil

1. In the mixing bowl mix up chopped okra, taco seasoning, and sunflower oil.
2. Then preheat the air fryer to 385F.
3. Put the okra mixture in the air fryer and cook it for 5 minutes.
4. Then shake the vegetables well and cook them for 5 minutes more.

Cumin Garlic

Prep time:5 minutes |Cook time: 10 minutes |Serves 4

- 2 garlic bulbs
- ½ teaspoon cumin seeds
- 1 teaspoon olive oil

1. In the shallow bowl mix up cumin seeds and olive oil.
2. Then brush the garlic bulbs with oil mixture and put them in the air fryer.
3. Cook the garlic for 10 minutes at 375F.

Green Bean Casserole

Prep time: 2 minutes | Cook time: 10 minutes | Serves 2

- tbsp. butter, melted
- 1 cup green beans
- 6 oz. cheddar cheese, shredded
- 7 oz. parmesan cheese, shredded
- ¼ cup heavy cream

1. Pre-heat your fryer at 400°F.

2. Take a baking dish small enough to fit inside the fryer and cover the bottom with melted butter. Throw in the green beans, cheddar cheese, and any seasoning as desired, then give it a stir. Add the parmesan on top and finally the heavy cream.
3. Cook in the fryer for six minutes. Allow to cool before serving.

Carrots with Sesame Seeds

Prep time: 20 minutes | Cook time:15 minutes |Serves 3

- 3/4 pound carrots, trimmed and cut into sticks
- 2 tablespoons butter, melted
- Coarse sea salt and white pepper, to taste
- 1 tablespoon sesame seeds, lightly toasted

1. Toss the carrots with the butter, salt, and white pepper | then, arrange them in the Air Fryer basket.
2. Cook the carrots at 380 °F for 15 minutes | make sure to check the carrots halfway through the cooking time.
3. Top the carrots with the sesame seeds. Bon appétit!

Butter Garlic Brussels Sprouts

Prep time: 15 minutes | Cook time:14 minutes |Serves 3

- 3/4 pound Brussels sprouts
- 2 tablespoons butter, melted
- 2 garlic cloves, crushed
- Kosher salt and ground black pepper, to taste

1. Toss the Brussels sprouts with the remaining ingredients until well coated.
2. Arrange the Brussels sprouts in the Air Fryer basket.
3. Cook the Brussels sprouts at 380 °F for 14 minutes, shaking the basket halfway through the cooking time.
4. Bon appétit!

Garlicky and Lemony Mushrooms

Prep time: 12 minutes | Cook time:11 minutes |Serves 3

- 3/4 pound button mushrooms, cleaned and cut into halves
- 2 tablespoons olive oil
- 1 garlic clove, pressed
- Sea salt and ground black pepper, to taste
- 1 tablespoon fresh lemon juice
- 1 tablespoon fresh cilantro, chopped

1. Toss your mushrooms with the olive oil, garlic, salt, and black pepper.
2. Arrange them on a lightly oiled Air Fryer basket.
3. Air fry the mushrooms at 375 °F for about 11 minutes, shaking the basket halfway through the cooking time.
4. Drizzle fresh lemon juice over the mushroom and serve with the fresh cilantro. Enjoy!

Paprika Sweet Potatoes

Prep time: 40 minutes | Cook time:35 minutes |Serves 4

- 1 pound sweet potatoes, scrubbed and halved
- 3 tablespoons olive oil
- 1 teaspoon paprika
- Sea salt and ground black pepper, to taste

1. Toss the sweet potatoes with the olive oil, paprika, salt, and black pepper.
2. Cook the sweet potatoes at 380 °F for 35 minutes, shaking the basket halfway through the cooking time.
3. Taste and adjust the seasonings. Bon appétit!

Broccoli Salad

Prep time: 3 minutes | Cook time: 12 minutes | Serves 2

- 3 cups fresh broccoli florets
- 2 tbsp. coconut oil, melted
- ¼ cup sliced s
- ½ medium lemon, juiced

1. Take a six-inch baking dish and fill with the broccoli florets. Pour the melted coconut oil over the broccoli and add in the sliced s. Toss together. Put the dish in the air fryer.
2. Cook at 380°F for seven minutes, stirring at the halfway point.
3. Place the broccoli in a bowl and drizzle the lemon juice over it.

Creamy Cauliflower

Prep time:10 minutes |Cook time: 12 minutes
|Serves 4

- 1-pound cauliflower
- 1 teaspoon taco seasonings
- 1 tablespoon heavy cream
- 1 teaspoon olive oil

1. Chop the cauliflower roughly and sprinkle it with taco seasonings and heavy cream.
2. Then sprinkle the cauliflower with olive oil.
3. Preheat the air fryer to 400F.
4. Cook it for 12 minutes.
5. Shake the vegetables every 3 minutes.

Saucy Brown Mushrooms

Prep time: 9 minutes | Cook time:7 minutes
|Serves 4

- 1 pound brown mushrooms, quartered
- 2 tablespoons sesame oil
- 1 tablespoon tamari sauce
- 1 garlic clove, pressed
- Sea salt and ground black pepper, to taste

1. Toss the mushrooms with the remaining ingredients. Toss until they are well coated on all sides.
2. Arrange the mushrooms in the Air Fryer basket.
3. Cook your mushrooms at 400 °F for about 7 minutes, shaking the basket halfway through the cooking time.
4. Bon appétit!

Butter Broccoli

Prep time:5 minutes |Cook time: 15 minutes
|Serves 4

- 1 pound broccoli florets Apinch of salt and black pepper

- 1 teaspoons sweet paprika
- ½ tablespoon butter, melted

1. In a bowl, mix the broccoli with the rest of the ingredients, and toss.
2. Put the broccoli in your air fryer's basket, cook at 350 °F for 15 minutes, divide between plates and serve.

Classic Broccoli Florets

Prep time: 8 minutes | Cook time:6 minutes
|Serves 3

- 3/4 pound broccoli florets
- 1 tablespoon olive oil
- 1 teaspoon garlic powder
- Sea salt and ground black pepper, to taste

1. Toss the broccoli florets with the remaining ingredients until well coated.
2. Arrange the broccoli florets in the Air Fryer basket.
3. Cook the broccoli florets at 395 °F for 6 minutes, shaking the basket halfway through the cooking time.
4. Bon appétit!

Cabbage Steaks

Prep time: 2 minutes | Cook time: 5 minutes | Serves 2

- small head cabbage
- 1 tsp. butter, butter
- 1 tsp. paprika
- 1 tsp. olive oil

1. Halve the cabbage.
2. In a bowl, mix together the melted butter, paprika, and olive oil. Massage into the cabbage slices, making sure to coat it well. Season as desired with salt and pepper or any other seasonings of your choosing.
3. Pre-heat the fryer at 400°F and set the rack inside.
4. Put the cabbage in the fryer and cook for three minutes. Flip it and cook on the other side for another two minutes. Enjoy!

Classic Spicy Potatoes

Prep time: 20 minutes | Cook time:13 minutes | Serves 4

- 1 pound potatoes, diced into bite-sized chunks
- 1 tablespoon olive oil
- Sea salt and ground black pepper, to taste
- 1 teaspoon chili powder

1. Toss the potatoes with the remaining ingredients until well coated on all sides.
2. Arrange the potatoes in the Air Fryer basket.
3. Cook the potatoes at 400 °F for about 13 minutes, shaking the basket halfway through the cooking time.
4. Bon   appétit!

Cajun Peppers

Prep time:4 minutes |Cook time: 12 minutes |Serves 4

- 1 tablespoon olive oil
- ½ pound mixed bell peppers, sliced
- 1 cup black olives, pitted and halved
- ½ tablespoon Cajun seasoning

1. In a pan that fits the air fryer, combine all the ingredients.
2. Put the pan it in your air fryer and cook at 390 °F for 12 minutes.
3. Divide the mix between plates and serve.

Cheesy Kale

Prep time: 3 minutes | Cook time: 12 minutes | Serves 2

- lb. kale
- 8 oz. parmesan cheese, shredded
- 1 onion, diced
- 1 tsp. butter
- 1 cup heavy cream

1. Dice up the kale, discarding any hard stems. In a baking dish small enough to fit inside the fryer, combine the kale with the parmesan, onion, butter and cream.
2. Pre-heat the fryer at 250°F.
3. Set the baking dish in the fryer and cook for twelve minutes. Make sure to give it a good stir before serving.

Cheddar Asparagus

Prep time:5 minutes |Cook time: 10 minutes |Serves 4

- 2 pounds asparagus, trimmed
- 2 tablespoons olive oil
- 1 cup cheddar cheese, shredded
- 4 garlic cloves, minced
- 4 bacon slices, cooked and crumbled

1. In a bowl, mix the asparagus with the other ingredients except the bacon, toss and put in your air fryer's basket.
2. Cook at 400 °F for 10 minutes, divide between plates, sprinkle the bacon on top and serve.

Mozzarella Asparagus Mix

Prep time:5 minutes |Cook time: 10 minutes |Serves 4

- 1 pound asparagus, trimmed
- 2 tablespoons olive oil Apinch of salt and black pepper
- 2 cups mozzarella, shredded
- ½ cup balsamic vinegar
- 2 cups cherry tomatoes, halved

1. In a pan that fits your air fryer, mix the asparagus with the rest of the ingredients except the mozzarella and toss.
2. Put the pan in the air fryer and cook at 400 °F for 10 minutes.
3. Divide between plates and serve.

Chapter 8

Desserts

Almond Cookies

Prep time:5 minutes |Cook time: 15 minutes |Serves 8

- 1 and ½ cups almonds, crushed
- 2 tablespoons erythritol
- ½ teaspoon baking powder
- ¼ teaspoon almond extract
- 2 eggs, whisked

1. In a bowl, mix all the ingredients and whisk well.
2. Scoop 8 servings of this mix on a baking sheet that fits the air fryer which you've lined with parchment paper.
3. Put the baking sheet in your air fryer and cook at 350 ˚F for 15 minutes.
4. Serve cold.

Almond Bars

Prep time:5 minutes |Cook time: 12 minutes |Serves 12

- 1 teaspoon vanilla extract
- 1 cup almond butter, soft
- 1 egg
- 2 tablespoons erythritol

1. In a bowl, mix all the ingredients and whisk really well.
2. Spread this on a baking sheet that fits the air fryer lined with parchment paper, introduce in the fryer and cook at 350 ˚F and bake for 12 minutes.
3. Cool down, cut into bars and serve.

Sugar Pork Rinds

Prep time: 3 minutes | Cook time: 10 minutes | Serves 2

- 2 oz. pork rinds
- 2 tsp. unsalted butter, melted
- ¼ cup powdered erythritol
- ½ tsp. ground cinnamon

1. Coat the rinds with the melted butter.
2. In a separate bowl, combine the erythritol and cinnamon and pour over the pork rinds, ensuring the rinds are covered completely and evenly.
3. Transfer the pork rinds into the fryer and cook at 400°F for five minutes.

Baked Plum Cream

Prep time:5 minutes |Cook time: 20 minutes |Serves 4

- 1 pound plums, pitted and chopped
- ¼ cup swerve
- 1 tablespoon lemon juice
- 1 and ½ cups heavy cream

1. In a bowl, mix all the ingredients and whisk really well.
2. Divide this into 4 ramekins, put them in the air fryer and cook at 340 ˚F for 20 minutes.
3. Serve cold.

Peanut Cookies

Prep time:15 minutes |Cook time: 5 minutes |Serves 4

- 4 tablespoons peanut butter
- 4 teaspoons Erythritol
- 1 egg, beaten
- ¼ teaspoon vanilla extract

1. In the mixing bowl mix up peanut butter, Erythritol, egg, and vanilla extract.
2. Stir the mixture with the help of the fork.
3. Then make 4 cookies.
4. Preheat the air fryer to 355F.
5. Place the cookies in the air fryer and cook them for 5 minutes.

Lemon Berry Jam

Prep time:10 minutes |Cook time: 20 minutes |Serves 12

- ¼ cup swerve
- 8 ounces strawberries, sliced
- 1 tablespoon lemon juice
- ¼ cup water

1. In a pan that fits the air fryer, combine all the ingredients, put the pan in the machine and cook at 380 °F for 20 minutes.
2. Divide the mix into cups, cool down and serve.

Fried Banana S'mores

Prep time: 5 minutes | Cook time:6 minutes |Serves 4

- 4 bananas
- 3 tablespoons mini semi-sweet chocolate chips
- 3 tablespoons mini peanut butter chips
- 3 tablespoons mini marshmallows
- 3 tablespoons graham cracker cereal

1. Pre-heat the air fryer to 400°F.
2. Slice into the un-peeled bananas lengthwise along the inside of the curve, but do not slice through the bottom of the peel. Open the banana slightly to form a pocket.
3. Fill each pocket with chocolate chips, peanut butter chips and marshmallows. Poke the graham cracker cereal into the filling.
4. Place the bananas in the air fryer basket, resting them on the side of the basket and each other to keep them upright with the filling facing up. Air-fry for 6 minutes, or until the bananas are soft to the touch, the peels have blackened and the chocolate and marshmallows

have melted and toasted.

5. Let them cool for a couple of minutes and then simply serve with a spoon to scoop out the filling.

Swedish Chocolate Mug Cake

Prep time: 3 minutes | Cook time: 12 minutes | Serves 1

- 1 tbsp. cocoa powder
- 3 tbsp. coconut oil
- ¼ cup flour
- 3 tbsp. whole milk
- 5 tbsp. sugar

1. In a bowl, stir together all of the ingredients to combine them completely.
2. Take a short, stout mug and pour the mixture into it.
3. Put the mug in your Air Fryer and cook for 10 minutes at 390°F.

Roasted Bourbon Cherries

Prep time: 25 minutes | Cook time: 20 minutes |Serves 4

- 2 cups cherries, pitted
- 4 tablespoons brown sugar
- 1 tablespoon coconut oil
- 2 tablespoons bourbon
- 1/4 teaspoon ground cinnamon

1. Toss the cherries with the remaining ingredients | place your cherries in a lightly greased baking dish.
2. Roast the cherries in the preheated Air Fryer at 370 °F for approximately 20 minutes.
3. Serve at room temperature. Bon appétit!

Pineapple Sticks

Prep time: 3 minutes | Cook time: 17 minutes | Serves 4

- ½ fresh pineapple, cut into sticks
- ¼ cup desiccated coconut

1. Pre-heat the Air Fryer to 400°F.
2. Coat the pineapple sticks in the desiccated coconut and put each one in the Air Fryer basket.
3. Air fry for 10 minutes.

Banana Oatmeal Cookies

Prep time: 3 minutes | Cook time: 20 minutes | Serves 6

- 2 cups quick oats
- ¼ cup milk
- 4 ripe bananas, mashed
- ¼ cup coconut, shredded

1. Pre-heat the Air Fryer to 350°F.
2. Combine all of the ingredients in a bowl.

3. Scoop equal amounts of the cookie dough onto a baking sheet and put it in the Air Fryer basket.
4. Bake the cookies for 15 minutes.

Traditional Danish Pastry

Prep time: 25 minutes | Cook time:20 minutes |Serves 5

- 12 ounces refrigerated puff pastry
- 1 cup apple pie filling

1. Roll out the puff pastry sheet into a large rectangle | cut the pastry sheet into triangles.
2. Spoon the filling into each triangle | fold the pastry over and seal the edges with your fingers.
3. Bake the Danish pastry at 350 °F for 20 minutes or until the top is golden brown. Bon appétit!

Cocoa Bombs

Prep time:5 minutes |Cook time: 8 minutes |Serves 12

- 2 cups macadamia nuts, chopped
- 4 tablespoons coconut oil, melted
- 1 teaspoon vanilla extract
- ¼ cup cocoa powder
- 1/3 cup swerve

1. In a bowl, mix all the ingredients and whisk well.
2. Shape medium balls out of this mix, place them in your air fryer and cook at 300 °F for 8 minutes.
3. Serve cold.

Berry Layer Cake

Prep time: 2 minutes | Cook time: 8 minutes | Serves 1

- ¼ lemon pound cake
- ¼ cup whipping cream
- ½ tsp Truvia
- 1/8 tsp orange flavor
- 1 cup of mixed berries

1. Using a sharp knife, divide the lemon cake into small cubes.
2. Dice the strawberries.
3. Combine the whipping cream, Truvia, and orange flavor.
4. Layer the fruit, cake and cream in a glass.
5. Serve!

Coffee Surprise

Prep time: 2 minutes | Cook time: 5 minutes | Serves 1

- 2 heaped tbsp flaxseed, ground
- 100ml cooking cream 35% fat
- ½ tsp cocoa powder, dark and unsweetened
- 1 tbsp goji berries
- Freshly brewed coffee

1. Mix together the flaxseeds, cream and cocoa and coffee.
2. Season with goji berries.
3. Serve!

Banana Chia Seed Pudding

Prep time: 5 minutes | Cook time: 1-2 days | Serves 1

- 1 can full-fat coconut milk
- 1 medium- or small-sized banana, ripe
- ½ tsp cinnamon
- 1 tsp vanilla extract
- ¼ cup chia seeds

1. In a bowl, mash the banana until soft.

2. Add the remaining ingredients and mix until incorporated.
3. Cover and place in your refrigerator overnight.
4. Serve!

Lemon Berries Stew

Prep time:10 minutes |Cook time: 20 minutes |Serves 4

- 1 pound strawberries, halved
- 4 tablespoons stevia
- 1 tablespoon lemon juice
- 1 and ½ cups water

1. In a pan that fits your air fryer, mix all the ingredients, toss, put it in the fryer and cook at 340 °F for 20 minutes.
2. Divide the stew into cups and serve cold.

Cheesecake Cups

Prep time: 2 minutes | Cook time: 10 minutes | Serves 4

- 8 oz cream cheese, softened
- 2 oz heavy cream
- 1 tsp Sugar Glycerite
- 1 tsp Splenda
- 1 tsp vanilla flavoring (Frontier Organic)

1. Combine all the ingredients.
2. Whip until a pudding consistency is achieved.
3. Divide in cups.
4. Refrigerate until served!

Classic Cinnamon Donuts

Prep time: 20 minutes | Cook time: 20 minutes |Serves 4

- 12 ounces flaky large biscuits
- 1/4 cup granulated sugar
- 1 teaspoon ground cinnamon
- 1/4 teaspoon grated nutmeg
- 2 tablespoons coconut oil

1. Separate the dough into biscuits and place them in a lightly oiled Air Fryer cooking basket.
2. Mix the sugar, cinnamon, nutmeg, and coconut oil until well combined.
3. Drizzle your donuts with the cinnamon mixture.
4. Bake your donuts in the preheated Air Fryer at 340 °F for approximately 10 minutes or until golden. Repeat with the remaining donuts.
5. Bon   appétit!

Toasted Coconut Flakes

Prep time: 2 minutes | Cook time: 5 minutes | Serves 1

- 1 cup unsweetened coconut flakes
- 2 tsp. coconut oil, melted
- ¼ cup granular erythritol
- Salt

1. In a large bowl, combine the coconut flakes, oil, granular erythritol, and a pinch of salt, ensuring that the flakes are coated completely.
2. Place the coconut flakes in your fryer and cook at 300°F for three minutes, giving the basket a good shake a few times throughout the cooking time. Fry until golden and serve.

Cream Cups

Prep time:5 minutes |Cook time: 10 minutes |Serves 6

- 2 tablespoons butter, melted
- 8 ounces cream cheese, soft
- 3 tablespoons coconut, shredded and unsweetened
- 3 eggs
- 4 tablespoons swerve

1. In a bowl, mix all the ingredients and whisk really well.
2. Divide into small ramekins, put them in the fryer and cook at 320 °F and bake for 10 minutes.
3. Serve cold.

Currant Cream Ramekins

Prep time:5 minutes |Cook time: 20 minutes |Serves 6

- 1 cup red currants, blended
- 1 cup black currants, blended
- 3 tablespoons stevia
- 1 cup coconut cream

1. In a bowl, combine all the ingredients and stir well.
2. Divide into ramekins, put them in the fryer and cook at 340 °F for 20 minutes.
3. Serve the pudding cold.

Appendix 1 Measurement Conversion Chart

Volume Equivalents (Dry)

US STANDARD	METRIC (APPROXIMATE)
1/8 teaspoon	0.5 mL
1/4 teaspoon	1 mL
1/2 teaspoon	2 mL
3/4 teaspoon	4 mL
1 teaspoon	5 mL
1 tablespoon	15 mL
1/4 cup	59 mL
1/2 cup	118 mL
3/4 cup	177 mL
1 cup	235 mL
2 cups	475 mL
3 cups	700 mL
4 cups	1 L

Volume Equivalents (Liquid)

US STANDARD	US STANDARD (OUNCES)	METRIC (AP-PROXIMATE)
2 tablespoons	1 fl.oz.	30 mL
1/4 cup	2 fl.oz.	60 mL
1/2 cup	4 fl.oz.	120 mL
1 cup	8 fl.oz.	240 mL
1 1/2 cup	12 fl.oz.	355 mL
2 cups or 1 pint	16 fl.oz.	475 mL
4 cups or 1 quart	32 fl.oz.	1 L
1 gallon	128 fl.oz.	4 L

Temperatures Equivalents

FAHRENHEIT(F)	CELSIUS(C) APPROXIMATE)
225 °F	107 °C
250 °F	120 ° °C
275 °F	135 °C
300 °F	150 °C
325 °F	160 °C
350 °F	180 °C
375 °F	190 °C
400 °F	205 °C
425 °F	220 °C
450 °F	235 °C
475 °F	245 °C
500 °F	260 °C

Weight Equivalents

US STANDARD	METRIC (APPROXIMATE)
1 ounce	28 g
2 ounces	57 g
5 ounces	142 g
10 ounces	284 g
15 ounces	425 g
16 ounces (1 pound)	455 g
1.5 pounds	680 g
2 pounds	907 g

Appendix 2 The Dirty Dozen and Clean Fifteen

The Environmental Working Group (EWG) is a nonprofit, nonpartisan organization dedicated to protecting human health and the environment Its mission is to empower people to live healthier lives in a healthier environment. This organization publishes an annual list of the twelve kinds of produce, in sequence, that have the highest amount of pesticide residue-the Dirty Dozen-as well as a list of the fifteen kinds of produce that have the least amount of pesticide residue-the Clean Fifteen.

THE DIRTY DOZEN

The 2016 Dirty Dozen includes the following produce. These are considered among the year's most important produce to buy organic:

Strawberries	Spinach
Apples	Tomatoes
Nectarines	Bell peppers
Peaches	Cherry tomatoes
Celery	Cucumbers
Grapes	Kale/collard greens
Cherries	Hot peppers

The Dirty Dozen list contains two additional itemskale/collard greens and hot peppers-because they tend to contain trace levels of highly hazardous pesticides.

THE CLEAN FIFTEEN

The least critical to buy organically are the Clean Fifteen list. The following are on the 2016 list:

Avocados	Papayas
Corn	Kiw
Pineapples	Eggplant
Cabbage	Honeydew
Sweet peas	Grapefruit
Onions	Cantaloupe
Asparagus	Cauliflower
Mangos	

Some of the sweet corn sold in the United States are made from genetically engineered (GE) seedstock. Buy organic varieties of these crops to avoid GE produce.

Appendix 3 Index

Barbara W. Bolick

Printed in Great Britain
by Amazon

33381562R00042